*Masonic Symbolism
of King Solomon's Temple*

By Albert G. Mackey, H. L. Haywood,
Frank C. Higgins, David Harlow
and Robert Smailes

Copyright © 2020 Lamp of Trismegistus. All rights reserved. No part of this publication may be reproduced or transmitted in any form or by any means, electronic or mechanical, including photocopying, recording, or by any information storage and retrieval system, without permission in writing from Lamp of Trismegistus. Reviewers may quote brief passages.

ISBN: 978-1-63118-442-0

*Foundations of Freemasonry
Series*

Other Books in this Series and Related Titles

Psalms of Solomon by King Solomon (978-1-63118-439-0)

A Few Masonic Sermons
by A. C. Ward & Bascom B. Clarke (978-1-63118-435-2)

Royal Arch, Capitular and Cryptic Masonry
by various authors (978-1-63118-425-3)

Masonic Symbolism of Easter and the Christ in Masonry
by various authors (978-1-63118-434-5)

Ancient Egyptian Mysteries and Hieroglyphics, Modern Freemasonry & Initiation of the Pyramid by various (978-1-63118-430-7)

The Two Great Pillars of Boaz and Jachin
by Albert Mackey, William Harvey & others (978-1-63118-433-8)

Masonic Symbolism of the Apron & the Altar
by various authors (978-1-63118-428-4)

Lost Chapters of the Book of Daniel and Related Writings
by Daniel (978-1-63118-417-8)

Cloud Upon the Sanctuary by K. Eckartshausen (978-1-63118-438-3)

Symbolism and Discourses on the Entered Apprentice, Fellowcraft and Master Mason Blue Lodge Degrees by various (978-1-63118-413-0)

The Lost Keys of Freemasonry or The Secret of Hiram Abiff
by Manly P. Hall (978-1-63118-427-7)

The Story and Legend of Hiram Abiff by William Harvey, Manly P. Hall & Albert G. Mackey (978-1-63118-411-6)

Ancient Mysteries & Secret Societies
by Manly P. Hall (978-1-63118-410-9)

Audio Versions are also Available on Audible and iTunes

Table of Contents

Introduction...7

The Symbolism of Solomon's Temple
by Albert G. Mackey...9

Solomon's Temple
by David Harlow...23

The Middle Chamber of Solomon's Temple
by H. L. Haywood...33

Esoteric Symbolism of King Solomon's Temple
by Frank C. Higgins...37

A Short Explanation of the Seal of Solomon
by Albert G. Mackey...47

King Solomon's Temple and the Story of the Third Degree
by Robert Smailes...51

Introduction

From the beginning of Modern Freemasonry's birthdate of 1717, the intelligentsia of humanity have found refuge for safe reflection within the walls of the fraternity. Masonic writers have produced a nearly incalculable amount of written musings on a multitude of esoteric and philosophical subjects, as they relate to the ancient mysteries that Freemasonry currently storehouses. Sadly, most of it appears to have sat largely unread, as American Freemasonry in particular, continues to transform itself into something that bears little resemblance to what it was originally designed to be. The true essence of Freemasonry is not that of blind patriotism or a single-minded national religion but one of Universal Brotherhood and altruism, designed for the betterment not just of its members but of society as a whole. In particular, for those who are not members of the fraternity, as Freemasonry has always acted as a beacon, to help guide humanity through darker times, with the hopes that one day we will collectively reach a truly enlightened age.

It's not uncommon for new members joining the fraternity to find little education within the walls of many modern lodges, in spite of so much written material available to the membership. Many older members are not simply uneducated with regards to real Masonic history and symbology, not to mention the vast arena of related subjects, but they are disinterested in all of it, as well.

Lamp of Trismegistus is doing its part to help preserve humanity's Masonic history by making some of these classics available to those students who are seeking to unearth the knowledge of these ancient colossi. As such, Lamp of Trismegistus offers its readers highlights of Masonic study, culled from a variety of authors and viewpoints, with the hope bringing education back into the fraternity. So, be sure to check out other titles in our *Foundations of Freemasonry Series* as well as our *Esoteric Classics, Theosophical Classics, Occult Fiction* and our *Christian Apocrypha Series*, and don't be afraid to let a little altruism into your own heart or even into your Lodge. You can also download the audio versions of most of these titles from iTunes or Audible.

The Symbolism of Solomon's Temple

By Albert G. Mackey

I have said that the operative art is symbolized—that is to say, used as a symbol—in the speculative science. Let us now inquire, as the subject of the present essay, how this is done in reference to a system of symbolism dependent for its construction on types and figures derived from the temple of Solomon, and which we hence call the "Temple Symbolism of Freemasonry."

Bearing in mind that speculative Masonry dates its origin from the building of King Solomon's temple by Jewish and Tyrian artisans, the first important fact that attracts the attention is, that the operative masons at Jerusalem were engaged in the construction of an earthly and material temple, to be dedicated to the service and worship of God—a house in which Jehovah was to dwell visibly by his Shekinah, and whence he was, by the Urim and Thummim, to send forth his oracles for the government and direction of his chosen people.

Now, the operative art having, *for us*, ceased, we, as speculative Masons, symbolize the labors of our predecessors by engaging in the construction of a spiritual temple in our hearts, pure and spotless, fit for the dwelling-place of Him who is the author of purity—where God is to be worshipped in spirit and in truth, and whence every evil thought and unruly passion is to be banished, as the sinner and the Gentile were excluded from the sanctuary of the Jewish temple.

This spiritualizing of the temple of Solomon is the first, the most prominent and most pervading of all the symbolic instructions of Freemasonry. It is the link that binds the operative and speculative divisions of the order. It is this which gives it its religious character. Take from Freemasonry its dependence on the temple, leave out of its ritual all reference to that sacred edifice, and to the legends connected with it, and the system itself must at once decay and die, or at best remain only as some fossilized bone, imperfectly to show the nature of the living body to which it once belonged.

Temple worship is in itself an ancient type of the religious sentiment in its progress towards spiritual elevation. As soon as a nation emerged, in the world's progress, out of Fetishism, or the worship of visible objects,—the most degraded form of idolatry,—its people began to establish a priesthood and to erect temples. The Scandinavians, the Celts, the Egyptians, and the Greeks, however much they may have differed in the ritual and the objects of their polytheistic worship, all were possessed of priests and temples. The Jews first constructed their tabernacle, or portable temple, and then, when time and opportunity permitted, transferred their monotheistic worship to that more permanent edifice which is now the subject of our contemplation. The mosque of the Mohammedan and the church or the chapel of the Christian are but embodiments of the same idea of temple worship in a simpler form.

The adaptation, therefore, of the material temple to a science of symbolism would be an easy, and by no means a novel task, to both the Jewish and the Tyrian mind. Doubtless, at its original conception, the idea was rude and unembellished, to be perfected and polished only by future aggregations of succeeding intellects. And yet no biblical scholar will venture to deny that there was, in the mode of building, and in all the circumstances connected with the construction of King Solomon's temple, an apparent design to establish a foundation for symbolism.

I propose now to illustrate, by a few examples, the method in which the speculative Masons have appropriated this design of King Solomon to their own use.

To construct his earthly temple, the operative mason followed the architectural designs laid down on the *trestle-board*, or tracing-board, or book of plans of the architect. By these he hewed and squared his materials; by these he raised his walls; by these he constructed his arches; and by these strength and durability, combined with grace and beauty, were bestowed upon the edifice which he was constructing.

The trestle-board becomes, therefore, one of our elementary symbols. For in the masonic ritual the speculative Mason is reminded that, as the operative artist erects his temporal building, in accordance with the rules and designs laid down on the trestle-board of the master-workman, so should he erect that spiritual building, of which the material is a type, in obedience to the rules and designs, the precepts and commands, laid down by the grand Architect of the universe, in those great books of nature and revelation, which constitute the spiritual trestle-board of every Freemason.

The trestle-board is, then, the symbol of the natural and moral law. Like every other symbol of the order, it is universal and tolerant in its application; and while, as Christian Masons, we cling with unfaltering integrity to that explanation which makes the Scriptures of both dispensations our trestle-board, we permit our Jewish and Mohammedan brethren to content themselves with the books of the Old Testament, or the Koran. Masonry does not interfere with the peculiar form or development of any one's religious faith. All that it asks is, that the interpretation of the symbol shall be according to what each one supposes to be the revealed will of his Creator. But so rigidly exacting is it that the symbol shall be preserved, and, in some rational way, interpreted, that it peremptorily excludes the Atheist from its communion, because, believing in no Supreme Being, no divine Architect, he must necessarily be without a spiritual trestle-board on which the designs of that Being may be inscribed for his direction.

But the operative mason required materials wherewith to construct his temple. There was, for instance, the *rough ashlar*—the stone in its rude and natural state—unformed and unpolished, as it had been lying in the quarries of Tyre from the foundation of the earth. This stone was to be hewed and squared, to be fitted and adjusted, by simple, but appropriate implements, until it became a *perfect ashlar*, or well-finished stone, ready to take its destined place in the building.

Here, then, again, in these materials do we find other

elementary symbols. The rough and unpolished stone is a symbol of man's natural state—ignorant, uncultivated, and, as the Roman historian expresses it, "groveling to the earth, like the beasts of the field, and obedient to every sordid appetite;" but when education has exerted its salutary influences in expanding his intellect, in restraining his hitherto unruly passions, and purifying his life, he is then represented by the perfect ashlar, or finished stone, which, under the skillful hands of the workman, has been smoothed, and squared, and fitted for its appropriate place in the building.

Here an interesting circumstance in the history of the preparation of these materials has been seized and beautifully appropriated by our symbolic science. We learn from the account of the temple, contained in the First Book of Kings, that "The house, when it was in building, was built of stone, made ready before it was brought thither, so that there was neither hammer nor axe, nor any tool of iron, heard in the house while it was in building."

Now, this mode of construction, undoubtedly adopted to avoid confusion and discord among so many thousand workmen, has been selected as an elementary symbol of concord and harmony—virtues which are not more essential to the preservation and perpetuity of our own society than they are to that of every human association.

The perfect ashlar, therefore,—the stone thus fitted for its appropriate position in the temple,—becomes not only a symbol of human perfection (in itself, of course, only a comparative term), but also, when we refer to the mode in which it was prepared, of that species of perfection which results from the concord and union of men in society. It is, in fact, a symbol of the social character of the institution.

There are other elementary symbols, to which I may hereafter have occasion to revert; the three, however, already described,—the rough ashlar, the perfect ashlar, and the trestle-board,—and which, from their importance, have received the name of "jewels," will be sufficient to give some idea of the nature of what may be called the "symbolic alphabet" of Masonry. Let us now proceed to a brief consideration of the method in which this alphabet of the science is applied to the more elevated and abstruser portions of the system, and which, as the temple constitutes its most important type, I have chosen to call the "Temple Symbolism of Masonry."

Both Scripture and tradition inform us that, at the building of King Solomon's temple, the masons were divided into different classes, each engaged in different tasks. We learn, from the Second Book of Chronicles, that these classes were the bearers of burdens, the hewers of stones, and the overseers, called by the old masonic writers the *Ish sabal*, the *Ish chotzeb*, and the *Menatzchim*. Now, without pretending to say that the modern institution has preserved precisely the same system of regulations as that which was observed at the temple, we shall certainly find a similarity in these divisions to the Apprentices, Fellow Crafts and Master Masons of our own day. At all events, the three divisions made by King Solomon, in the workmen at Jerusalem, have been adopted as the types of the three degrees now practiced in speculative Masonry; and as such we are, therefore, to consider them. The mode in which these three divisions of workmen labored in constructing the temple, has been beautifully symbolized in speculative Masonry, and constitutes an important and interesting part of temple symbolism.

Thus we know, from our own experience among modern workmen, who still pursue the same method, as well as from the traditions of the order, that the implements used in the quarries were few and simple, the work there requiring necessarily, indeed, but two tools, namely, the *twenty-four inch gauge*, or two foot rule, and the *common gavel*, or stone-cutter's hammer. With the former implement, the operative mason took the necessary dimensions of the stone he was about to prepare, and with the latter, by repeated blows, skillfully applied, he broke off every unnecessary protuberance, and rendered it smooth and square, and fit to take its place in the building.

And thus, in the first degree of speculative Masonry, the Entered Apprentice receives these simple implements, as the emblematic working tools of his profession, with their appropriate symbolical instruction. To the operative mason their mechanical and practical use alone is signified, and nothing more of value does their presence convey to his mind. To the speculative Mason the sight of them is suggestive of far nobler and sublimer thoughts; they teach him to measure, not stones, but time; not to smooth and polish the marble for the builder's use, but to purify and cleanse his heart from every vice and imperfection that would render it unfit for a place in the spiritual temple of his body.

In the symbolic alphabet of Freemasonry, therefore, the twenty-four inch gauge is a symbol of time well employed; the common gavel, of the purification of the heart.

Here we may pause for a moment to refer to one of the coincidences between Freemasonry and those *Mysteries* which formed so important a part of the ancient religions, and which coincidences have led the writers on this subject to the formation of a well-supported theory that there was a common connection between them. The coincidence to which I at present allude is this: in all these Mysteries—the incipient ceremony of initiation—the first step taken by the candidate was a lustration or purification. The aspirant was not permitted to enter the sacred vestibule, or take any part in the secret formula of initiation, until, by water or by fire, he was emblematically purified from the corruptions of the world which he was about to leave behind. I need not, after this, do more than suggest the similarity of this formula, in principle, to a corresponding one in Freemasonry, where the first symbols presented to the apprentice are those which inculcate a purification of the heart, of which the purification of the body in the ancient Mysteries was symbolic.

We no longer use the bath or the fountain, because in our philosophical system the symbolization is more abstract, if I may use the term; but we present the aspirant with the *lambskin apron*, the *gauge*, and the *gavel*, as symbols of a spiritual purification. The design is the same, but the mode in which it is accomplished is different.

Let us now resume the connected series of temple symbolism.

At the building of the temple, the stones having been thus prepared by the workmen of the lowest degree (the Apprentices, as we now call them, the aspirants of the ancient Mysteries), we are informed that they were transported to the site of the edifice on Mount Moriah, and were there placed in the hands of another class of workmen, who are now technically called the Fellow Crafts, and who correspond to the Mystes, or those who had received the second degree of the ancient Mysteries. At this stage of the operative work more extensive and important labors were to be performed, and accordingly a greater amount of skill and knowledge was required of those to whom these labors were entrusted. The stones, having been prepared by the Apprentices (for hereafter, in speaking of the workmen of the temple, I shall use the equivalent appellations of the more modern Masons), were now to be deposited in their destined places in the building, and the massive walls were to be erected. For these purposes implements of a higher and more complicated character than the gauge and gavel were necessary. The *square* was required to fit the joints with sufficient accuracy, the *level* to run the courses in a horizontal line, and the *plumb* to erect the whole with due regard to perfect perpendicularity. This portion of the labor finds its symbolism in the second degree of the speculative science, and in applying this symbolism we still continue to refer to the idea of erecting a spiritual temple in the heart.

The necessary preparations, then, having been made in the first degree, the lessons having been received by which the aspirant is taught to commence the labor of life with the purification of the heart, as a Fellow Craft he continues the task by cultivating those virtues which give form and impression to the character, as well adapted stones give shape and stability to the building. And hence the "working tools" of the Fellow Craft are referred, in their symbolic application, to those virtues. In the alphabet of symbolism, we find the square, the level, and the plumb appropriated to this second degree. The square is a symbol denoting morality. It teaches us to apply the unerring principles of moral science to every action of our lives, to see that all the motives and results of our conduct shall coincide with the dictates of divine justice, and that all our thoughts, words, and deeds shall harmoniously conspire, like the well-adjusted and rightly-squared joints of an edifice, to produce a smooth, unbroken life of virtue.

The plumb is a symbol of rectitude of conduct, and inculcates that integrity of life and undeviating course of moral uprightness which can alone distinguish the good and just man. As the operative workman erects his temporal building with strict observance of that plumb-line, which will not permit him to deviate a hair's breadth to the right or to the left, so the speculative Mason, guided by the unerring principles of right and truth inculcated in the symbolic teachings of the same implement, is steadfast in the pursuit of truth, neither bending beneath the frowns of adversity nor yielding to the seductions of prosperity.

The level, the last of the three working tools of the operative craftsman, is a symbol of equality of station. Not that equality of civil or social position which is to be found only in the vain dreams of the anarchist or the Utopian, but that great moral and physical equality which affects the whole human race as the children of one common Father, who causes his sun to shine and his rain to fall on all alike, and who has so appointed the universal lot of humanity, that death, the leveler of all human greatness, is made to visit with equal pace the prince's palace and the peasant's hut.

Here, then, we have three more signs or hieroglyphics added to our alphabet of symbolism. Others there are in this degree, but they belong to a higher grade of interpretation, and cannot be appropriately discussed in an essay on temple symbolism only.

We now reach the third degree, the Master Masons of the modern science, and the Epopts, or beholders of the sacred things in the ancient Mysteries.

In the third degree the symbolic allusions to the temple of Solomon, and the implements of Masonry employed in its construction, are extended and fully completed. At the building of that edifice, we have already seen that one class of the workmen was employed in the preparation of the materials, while another was engaged in placing those materials in their proper position. But there was a third and higher class,—the master workmen,—whose duty it was to superintend the two other classes, and to see that the stones were not only duly prepared, but that the most exact accuracy had been observed in giving to them their true juxtaposition in the edifice. It was then only that the last and finishing labor was performed, and the cement was applied by these skillful workmen, to secure the materials in their appropriate places, and to unite the building in one enduring and connected mass. Hence the *trowel*, we are informed, was the most important, though of course not the only, implement in use among the master builders. They did not permit this last, indelible operation to be performed by any hands less skillful than their own. They required that the craftsmen should prove the correctness of their work by the square, level, and plumb, and test, by these unerring instruments, the accuracy of their joints; and, when satisfied of the just arrangement of every part, the cement, which was to give an unchangeable union to the whole, was then applied by themselves.

Hence, in speculative Masonry, the trowel has been assigned to the third degree as its proper implement, and the symbolic meaning which accompanies it has a strict and beautiful reference to the purposes for which it was used in the ancient temple; for as it was there employed "to spread the cement which united the building in one common mass," so is it selected as the symbol of brotherly love—that cement whose object is to unite our mystic association in one sacred and harmonious band of brethren.

Here, then, we perceive the first, or, as I have already called it, the elementary form of our symbolism—the adaptation of the terms, and implements, and processes of an operative art to a speculative science. The temple is now completed. The stones having been hewed, squared, and numbered in the quarries by the apprentices,—having been properly adjusted by the craftsmen, and finally secured in their appropriate places, with the strongest and purest cement, by the master builders,—the temple of King Solomon presented, in its finished condition, so noble an appearance of sublimity and grandeur as to well deserve to be selected, as it has been, for the type or symbol of that immortal temple of the body, to which Christ significantly and symbolically alluded when he said, "Destroy this temple, and in three days I will raise it up."

This idea of representing the interior and spiritual man by a material temple is so apposite in all its parts as to have occurred on more than one occasion to the first teachers of Christianity. Christ himself repeatedly alludes to it in other passages, and the eloquent and figurative St. Paul beautifully extends the idea in one of his Epistles to the Corinthians, in the following language: "Know ye not that ye are the temple of God, and that the spirit of God dwelleth in you?" And again, in a subsequent passage of the same Epistle, he reiterates the idea in a more positive form: "What, know ye not that your body is the temple of the Holy Ghost which is in you, which ye have of God, and ye are not your own?" And Dr. Adam Clarke, while commenting on this latter passage, makes the very allusions which have been the topic of discussion in the present essay. "As truly," says he, "as the living God dwelt in the Mosaic tabernacle and in the temple of Solomon, so truly does the Holy Ghost dwell in the souls of genuine Christians; and as the temple and all its *utensils* were holy, separated from all common and profane uses, and dedicated alone to the service of God, so the bodies of genuine Christians are holy, and should be employed in the service of God alone."

The idea, therefore, of making the temple a symbol of the body, is not exclusively masonic; but the mode of treating the symbolism by a reference to the particular temple of Solomon, and to the operative art engaged in its construction, is peculiar to Freemasonry. It is this which isolates it from all other similar associations. Having many things in common with the secret societies and religious Mysteries of antiquity, in this "temple symbolism" it differs from them all.

Solomon's Temple

By David Harlow

"The land of Israel," the Talmud states, "is situated in the center of the world, and Jerusalem in the center of the land of Israel, and the Temple in the center of Jerusalem, and the Holy of Holies in the center of the Temple, and the foundation stone on which the world was founded is situated in the front of the Ark."

Nearly every religion has claimed for its principal shrine a similar world-center, so that the Rabbinical statement has no greater significance, geographically, than the traditional accounts of other primitive peoples. Yet if we interpret it theologically, there is considerable truth in the assertion. Another passage in the same book thus figuratively reiterates the idea: "The world is like the eyeball of man; the white is the ocean that surrounds the world, the black is the world itself, and the pupil is Jerusalem, and the image in the pupil is the Temple."

This image of the Jewish Temple is still impressed upon the eye of the religious world, and though the crescent banner now waves over the site of Solomon's edifice the "mountain of the lord's house" is still "exalted above the hills," for temple, basilica and mosque which have successively crowned its summit have endeared it to Jew, Christian and Mohammedan.

The temple of Jehovah was always a "pillar of witness" to the stern monotheism of Israel's faith, and to it the world owes its preservation from barbarism, for had Judaism succumbed to the seductive polytheism of Greece the Mosaic code would have been lost and the sermon on the mount never have been uttered. Therefore the temple of Solomon has to the Biblical scholar and religious student a greater attraction than any other sacred structure of antiquity.

Our information regarding its style and decoration is very slight, although some writers have attempted to fully describe its construction and architectural arrangements. Many have confused the accounts of the three buildings, which successively rose over the threshing floor of Araunah and have merged into a description of the Solomonian edifice, while others have relied upon the vision of Ezekiel for a correct account of its plan and construction. Josephus cannot be relied upon entirely in this matter, as he lived 1,000 years after its foundation, and we can hardly expect him to be accurate in every particular; such account as he gives is but meager. The farther we get away from contemporary evidence the more difficult it becomes to ascertain the truth, and it therefore behooves us to sift the evidence and to select a witness least liable to err. The two versions in the Bible —Kings and Chronicles—vary considerably. The Chronicler is supposed to have compiled his work in the third century before Christ, while most scholars concur in dating the account in the book of Kings much earlier. In fact, it is generally conceded that the latter represents the narrative of an eyewitness or one who lived while the Solomonian temple was extant. His relation is certainly more in harmony with the construction of the period. According to his statement the temple was founded in the fourth year and finished in the eleventh year of Solomon's reign.

—oOo—

The building was constructed of stone, and faced the east. It was 60 cubits long, 20 cubits wide and 30 cubits high. The interior of the edifice was boarded with cedar, while cedar beams supported the roof. The ceiling was also of cedar, but the floor was planked with fir. The structure consisted of two chambers, the outer one being known as the "holy place," or "sanctuary," the inner one called "holy of holies," or "oracle." The former was 40 cubits long, the latter 20 cubits in length. Within the oracle were placed two gilded cherubim, each standing ten cubits high. Each had two wings, one of which touched the wall, the other overshadowed the ark. "There was nothing in the ark save the two tables of stone which Moses put there at Horeb."

The walls of both chambers were covered with engraved designs of cherubim, palms and flowers overlaid with gold. "Windows of narrow lights" were constructed in the upper part of the walls, so that air and light were freely admitted into the building. The oracle was separated from the sanctuary by a double door of olive wood carved with the same figures and forms as those which adorned the walls. The edifice had but one entrance. This was in front, being prefaced by a portico having a width of ten cubits and extending the entire width of the building. Within this porch stood two bronze pillars, one on either side of the approach, having capitals of the same material most beautifully worked.

Around the temple were built a number of chambers, three stories in height, whose beams rested upon ledges of the main structure. This method of construction gave to each ascending tier an increased breadth of one cubit. As each chamber was five cubits in height, the three stories were equal in height to one-half the edifice. Access to these rooms was gained by a staircase contained within the thickness of the southern wall. A court ran round three sides of the building, while the entire precincts were enclosed by a wall "built with three rows of hewed stone and a row of cedar beams."

This brief description of the Solomonian temple by a writer antedating all other narrators, portrays a structure simple in design and construction, and which is entirely in accord with the architecture of that age and region. It is also in harmony with the primitive cult of the Jahvistic priesthood, and the needs of the Israelitish nation. As Prof. Maspero says, "Compared with the magnificent monuments of Egypt and Chaldea, the work of Solomon was what the Hebrew kingdom appears to us among the empires of the ancient world—a little temple suited to a little people.

The same distinguished scholar also remarks that "the few Hebrew edifices, of which remains have come down to us, reveal a method of construction and decoration common in Egypt." M. Babelon, whose views reflect those of M. de Vogue, the greatest authority of Phoenician art, says, "The architecture and the interior ornaments were all Egyptian in style, like the Phoenician temples themselves." The celebrated archeologist, M. Perrot, and his collaborator, M. Chipiez, the famous architect, assert that the whole system of the temple architecture and ornament is Phoenician. They further state, "The only temple which still exists on the soil of Phoenicia is nothing more than the reduction of an Egyptian shrine adapted to the soil and habits of its new country."

It must be remembered that the Hebrews and Phoenicians were allied by race and religion, and as Israel had no national art, principally owing to the strictures of the Mosaic code which proscribed the delineation or representation of any living thing, it was natural that David should ask the assistance of his royal neighbor to the project of erecting at Jerusalem a temple to the God of Israel similar to that which existed in the country of Hiram. The promise made was fulfilled when Solomon was prepared to carry out the undertaking. The King of Tyre sent his skilled artisans and the famous "stone-squarers" from Gebal to co-operate with the woodmen and stone-cutters of Israel. Like the Pharaohs of Egypt, the Hebrew monarch levied an army of workmen from the "strangers within the land," sending some to Lebanon to assist in the felling of its famous firs and cedars, while others were employed as bearers of burden in the neighboring quarries where the limestone was obtained for the masonry.

—oOo—

It is probable a Phoenician architect designed the structure and supervised its erection. The finely dressed stones and the beautifully engraved woodwork, also the bronze vessels and utensils were doubtless the expressions of Phoenicia's best art, although the representations of living forms which covered the walls and doors of the building and also adorned the vessels and utensils, were contrary to the Sinaitic law. We can hardly conceive that the priesthood would willingly permit the existence of such designs in willful violation of the Mosaic code were it then operative, and their presence rather supports the theory that the book of the law had not yet been written. The religious ideas of the early Hebrews were analogous to the conceptions of the Phoenicians. "In the earliest times," says Canon Rawlinson, "the religious sentiment of the Phoenicians acknowledged only a single deity—a single mighty power, which was supreme over the whole universe." This power, called by the early Hebrews *El*, received the additional appellation of Adonai by them, while the Phoenicians used the name Baal—both meaning "lord" or "proprietor." The temple of the Tyrian god contained no image, his presence being symbolized by two columns, analogous to the twin pillars which stood within the porch of Solomon's edifice and the two tables of stone placed inside the ark.

Prof. Sayce remarks that "the great temple of Melkarth, which Hiram had just completed at Tyre, probably served as the model for the temple at Jerusalem." The reverend gentleman further states, "The central sanctuary became the royal chapel-rather than the temple of the national God, and its priests were the paid officials of the sovereign rather than the administrators and interpreters to the people of the divine law." The sacred structures of Babylonia and Egypt were of a similar nature, the various priests being state officials, with the king as chief pontiff. The Solomonian temple was not open to the public, and even the minor priests were denied access to the most holy place. The temple ritual differed from the public sacrifices and ablutions as much as the conceptions of the priesthood and upper classes were in marked contrast with the popular ideas.

Jehovah to the people was only a superior mortal, delighting in wars and other national undertakings! one who was feared and who had to be appeased by sacrifices like the gods of the neighboring nations. With the intelligent classes God was conceived as a supra-mundane being whose earthly dwelling place was Jerusalem, but whose throne was situated in the heavens.

—oOo—

The name of Deity in all religions has been treated with the greatest reverence as also with the most superstitious awe. Temples were dedicated to the "name." It was a part of deity and as inseparable from God and man as spirit and shadow. Solomon said "I propose to build an house unto the name of the Lord," and Jehovah exclaimed, "My name shall be there." The form of Jehovah is modern, not being older than about A. D. 1520, according to Prof. Haupt, and both spelling and pronunciation are at variance with the Hebrew rendering.

The true pronunciation of this ineffable name has for centuries been lost, the four consonants Y H V H forming the only certain characters known. One Jewish school maintained that the vowel points of Adonai should be used to give the correct sound, while another insisted that the true form demanded the vowel points of Elohim. Most Semitic scholars now write the name Yahveh, although it is generally conceded that Yahvay more closely approximates the ancient pronunciation. Prof. Hommel claims that the name is of South Arabian origin, being derived from the ancient verb hawaya—Heb., hayah—"to be, to come into existence," and that it belongs to the very earliest language of the Hebrews. He gives the meaning of the divine appellation as "the Existing one," but claims that its earlier form was Yah or Yahu, and that the primitive Western Semitic name for God was Ya or Ai. There may be some affinity between the last-mentioned name and the Babylonian Ai—heaven.

The conception of Jehovah grew with the development

of Israelitic thought. In the pre-exilic period the Hebrews were henotheistic in their views, but after the captivity they were pronounced monotheists. They returned to Jerusalem fired with a new ardor and animated by a loftier ideal. They were to spread the name of Jehovah among all nations and to acquaint them with his laws. Judaism well performed its mission; it kept the torch of monotheism burning during the long centuries of darkness which veiled all lands during Greek and Roman domination, and transmitted its light to Christianity and Islam. Today it was become the great luminary of Western thought and the pole-star of national progress.

The Middle Chamber of Solomon's Temple

By H. L. Haywood

The ascent toward a place representing the Middle Chamber of King Solomon's Temple is the outstanding ceremony of the Second Degree. Allow us to briefly examine the Middle Chamber itself, and with the truth of which it is a symbol.

That it is a symbol, and not a bit of history, there is every evidence to show. Sir Charles Warren, while Master of the Quatuor Coronati Lodge of Research, gave expression to the opinion of the best modern scholars in saying that, "There never was a Middle Chamber in the Temple. . . . As the Fellow Crafts were only employed during the building of the Temple, they could not have used this Chamber for the service mentioned [you will recall what this service is supposed to have been] even if it had existed. . . . Even if this Chamber had existed they would not have been allowed to desecrate it by use as a pay office."

Albert Mackey, one of the most conservative of Masonic writers, and who wrote his "Symbolism of Freemasonry" some twenty years before Brother Warren delivered his speech, took the same position. As we may read: "The whole legend is, in fact, an historical myth, in which the mystic number of the steps, the process of passing to the Chamber, and the wages there received, are inventions added to or ingrafted on the fundamental history contained in the sixth chapter of Kings, to inculcate important symbolic instructions relative to the principles of the order."

The passage in the Book of Kings, to which Mackey here refers, is in the authorized version of the Bible as follows: "They went up with winding stairs into the middle chamber." Modern Biblical scholarship has shown that the term here translated "chamber" really means a "story," and that there were three such stories on one side of the Temple composed of small rooms in which the priests kept their vestments, utensils, etc. That workmen were paid their wages in this middle story, or that Fellow Crafts were there prepared for a higher grade, there is not a hint in the record to show. This account of the matter, as Mackey has said, is "an historical myth."

A myth has been defined as "philosophy in the making." It is an allegorical piece of fiction designed to convey some abstract teaching. The purpose of our ceremonies is not to furnish truth rather than history, and that truth is nowise affected by the accuracy or inaccuracy of the narrative behind which it is veiled. To remember this in all connections will save one from those pitfalls of literalism into which so many Masonic students used to fall.

When understood purely as a symbol, the Middle Chamber stands for that place in life in which we receive the rewards of our endeavors. This is the broadest sense of it. Its narrower sense, as found in the Second Degree lecture, is that it represents the wages of education, of mental culture, for learning is described as the peculiar work of the Fellow Craft. Learning stores the mind with facts, preserves one from bigotry and superstition, offers to one the fellowships of great minds, quickens perception, strengthens the faculties, gives one, in short, a masterful intellect. It is into the possession of such riches as these that the Winding Stairs of the Liberal Arts and Sciences bring a man at last.

We may rejoice that William Preston gave this teaching so large a place in our lectures, for without it Masonry would have been wholly inadequate as a complete system of life. Ignorance is a sin, in most cases at least, and the sooner we thus regard it the better will it be for all of us, Masons and profane. In olden days when men had so few opportunities for learning it was inevitable that the common man should be ignorant; but in these days, with public schools, correspondence schools, cheap books and periodicals, and free libraries, a man who remains content with not possessing the best that has been thought and said in the world is wholly without excuse. Always and everywhere should men have in the house of life a winding stair of art and of science up which to climb into a middle chamber wherein to hold converse with the good and great of all ages!

Esoteric Symbolism of King Solomon's Temple

By Frank C. Higgins

In our F. C. degree is embodied far more particular reference to the subject of Israel's great and world-famous Temple than in either the preceding or the following degrees. Indeed, upon strict analysis, the F. C. degree serves as little more than a fitting prelude and climax to the soul-stirring imagery of the M.C. lecture, which Masons have ever united in declaring to be the most beautiful and impressive allocution in our entire ritual.

It was undoubtedly the work of an author of profound culture, possessed of deep insight into the ancient mysteries ; for it contains many allusions to facts long since relegated to oblivion in a language the very ingenuousness of which is a marvelous subtlety, and, while seemingly but a relation of prosaic historical facts, is in reality one of the greatest metaphysical documents in the language of any time or place.

The three principal contemplations of the ancient philosophical mind were God, the Universe, Man. The supreme science of the universe viewed physical, Man as at once the Temple of God and the home of spiritual Man; thus investing the human individual with the same responsible stewardship that any master might reasonably exact from the servant, whose duty it was to keep his residence pure and undefiled.

The teaching of salutary truths has ever been best accomplished, according to oriental ideas, in the form of picturesque allegories and imageries which take hold upon the imaginations of the young and serve an admirable purpose in fixing upon the mind important truths, dissimulated to the "profane," but intense in meaning and purpose to the initiate. The sacred books of the world have all without exception been composed with this end in view.

Ask the time-occupied, busy, average Mason if he believes every word of the thrilling story with which he is made so familiar in the Lodge. He will frankly tell you no. "Part of it," he will say, "is true," because he can point to the literary source from which it is taken. "The rest," he will tell you, "may not be historically precise; but it is invaluable because of its efficiency in driving home and clenching the necessary moral lesson."

In these words he will be uttering a perfect description of the method pursued by the moral teachers of the ancient world, practically without exception. The western world is densely oblivious of the fact that a vast system of dissimulation of natural truths was begun at a remote date, by the priestly caste. Multitudes were unable to seize the idea of "reality" upon a purely spiritual plane. They could grasp only with the senses, just as the education in liberality of very young children begins with Santa Claus, who later proves to be "only Papa."

The considerations involved are too extensive to be adequately treated in a short commentary. They cover almost the entire domain of philosophy and metaphysics; but we venture a thought or so that may be helpful to the reverent seeker after "more light" who hesitates to enter the door of initiation because of a highly commendable fear that he may be taking a plunge into some unrealized profanation.

We need have no moral compunction about rereading the secular histories of most of the ancient nations, as those transmitted to us by the Greek historians of the Ptolemaic and Selucid periods of Egypt and Syria are shown by modern research to have been glaringly inaccurate as to the details of persons and events, although still carrying enough of such truth as had become traditional, to have a corroborative value in instances. The scholarship of the last century has recovered so much of the genuine history of the classic peoples, from their own records and monuments, as completely to destroy the value of those fantastic compilations (Berosus and Manetho, for instance) upon which many early 19th century biblical commentaries were constructed.

The entire pantheons of the ancient culture nations were composed of the attributes or emanations of a single, unrevealed, omnipotent Deity, considered as "Intelligences," and therefore possessing a species of individual Ego, controlled by the great central Power.

These divine intelligences were, for more complete realization, distributed throughout the solar system, when the incessant revolution and ever changing aspects of the latter became the basis of a great cosmic drama, so that the loves and hates, the wars and friendly gatherings, of the "gods" (Elohim) might be described in anthropomorphisms, or terms pertaining to the affairs of men. The initiate alone, through all the ages, possessed the key to this sacred science of secrecy, and stood in the breach between the untutored masses and their superstitious regard for the powers of Nature.

Generation upon generation of ancient hierophants knew that by "Hercules" was meant the planet Mercury at the moments of its numerous passages through the Solar corona, at which periods it became draped in the lion's skin; yet they con- structed an elaborate genealogy for the kings of Macedon which shows them to have been lineally descended from Hercules and Dejanira. Similar pedigrees were enjoyed by all the monarchs of old, especially the Egyptian Pharaohs, who were all sons of the sun god Ra, so that the analogous claims of the emperors of China and Japan in our own day are not without ample precedent. Alexander the Great of Macedon is always shown on his coins and monuments wearing a lion's skin as headdress, in honor of this peculiar parentage.

With reference to this widespread system of mystic theology, two facts may be established by any careful student.

The ever-recurrent course of universal nature being the basis upon which all arguments, however picturesque, are erected, the details are everywhere the same.

The sacred vocabularies of western peoples are mainly composed of translations and corruptions of eastern names and terms, largely Phoenician and Egyptian, showing the direction traveled.

In our western world we have the- completed spiritual edifice of our own Great Light, sufficing for all our present needs; but it also has its archeology, and those few of us who have the time and patience to go back and delve into what are commonly called the "Fathers of the Church" and into the grand old Talmud of Israel, and even do not stop until we reach the rude symbols of spiritual insight away back in the Bronze Age, are rewarded by the view of an infinity of constructive material which the hand of Time has cleared away,-the rubbish of our Temple.

It has been necessary to dwell upon these details in order to make manifest the process by which living men became mythical heroes and their memories draped in the, splendors of the universe. Man was endowed with a threefold constitution. His soul was a spark of the unrevealed Divinity, his spirit was bestowed upon him by the particular planet under the influence of which, according to the astrologer, he entered the realm of matter, while his body was an accretion of the elements, suspended in zones between the earth and the heavens. Thus the very kingship of the King determined his identity with the

Sun, and his panegyrists did not hesitate so to blend the human and divine, the natural and supernatural, that we are today speechless in wonder before the more than remarkable character of Solomon, the Sun King-a character historical without doubt, but elaborated upon until its glory has extended to the "uttermost parts of the earth."

We have, during the last century, recovered the entire and unbroken chronology of the Assyrian and Babylonian monarchies. The records of these ancient peoples consist in several instances of complete libraries made up of thousands of clay tablets, containing not only tradition and history, extending back to approximately B.C. 4500, verified by accounts of astronomical phenomena occurring in different reigns, by which modern savants. are able to fix dates to the very hour and minute, but also dictionaries, works on mathematics, syllabaries, by which the dead Sumerian and Akkadian writings could be translated into Babylonian, and elaborate records of the dealings of the kings of these countries with surrounding nations.

In not one single instance is there the slightest trace or track of an allusion to either a Hebrew nation prior to B.C. 925, or kings named David and Solomon at all.

According to the Hebrew record, these monarchs flourished about B.C. 1000-1100, which would render them contemporary with Kings Marduk-Nadin-Akhi, Marduk-Shapik-Zerim, and Ramman-apil-iddina of the first Babylonian empire and Tiglath-Pileser I, Shamshi-Ramman I, and Ashur-

Bel-Kala of Assyria. As to Egypt, the biblical Solomonic period lies parallel to that of the later Ramesside kings of Thebes, and precedes that of Shi-shank of Bubastis, whose inscription on the walls of the great Temple of Karnak, including the "King of Judah" among the list of his prisoners in an expedition, is the first secular reference to the latter people. This king is presumed to have been Rehoboam, whose father and grandfather were the individual monarchs immortalized under the names of "David" and "Solomon." Jehu, king of Israel in the reign of King Shalmanesar II, of Assyria, was the first biblical monarch whose name was actually recorded on a contemporary monument (B.C. 800). It is a long-forgotten fact that all the ancient Hebrew names, beginning with the ineffable Tetragrammaton, are cabalistic constructions, upon a system borrowed from the Chaldeans, who were an equally Semitic people and the rootstock of the Abramic tribes.

Not only was each of the 22 letters of the Hebrew alphabet a number, so that geometrical and mathematical formulas expressed in letters became words, but the three Hebrew letters A, M, and Sh represented the elements air, water, and fire respectively; Ch, V, H, Z, Th, Y, L, N, S, O, Q, Tz, the 12 signs of the zodiac, beginning with Aries, and G, B, D, K, P, R, T, the menorah or Saturn, Jupiter, Mars, Sun, Venus, Mercury, and the Moon. Thus all the possible astronomical aspects of the heavens either spelled words already known or suggested new ones.

The name "Solomon" is as completely cabalistic as the powers attributed to the great founder of our craft; but it antedates its use as that of Israel's king, for we have a king of Assyria at B.C. 1300 named Shalmanesar, the construction of whose name, from "S-L-M-N" and the word "sar," meaning king," is as unequivocally "King Solomon" as the latter in English.

Why then were these letters employed? No one can fail to find them aligned in the Hebrew alphabet, as representative of the values 60, 30, 40, 50, the sum total of which is 180, or the semicircle of the sun's daily journey from east to west and nightly voyage through the underworld from west to east. It also represents the passage of the sun from the sign of Leo the lion, through Virgo, Libra, Scorpio, and Sagittarius, causing it to describe the Royal Arch, of which Libra, the highest of the 12 signs, constituted the Keystone from B.C. 1835 to A.D. 325. This passage, through five signs, constitutes the completion of each year's symbolic Temple to the Author and Giver of All Good, represented by the element "Fire," the Earth sign Taurus (corresponding to the letter A as well as V-Aleph, an Ox) and two signs of Gemini in each case suggesting the analogy between Hercules and Apollo (Tammuz or Adonis) of later eschatology, and the two sons of David,-Jedediah ("God's Strength") and Adonijah ("God's Love"). Hercules, as the Tyrian Melkarth (Melek-Kartha), was Hermes "King of the City" (of Tyre), and Apollo Hermes, the Divine Wisdom, who accompanies the Sun, the nearest of all his planetary retinue, until in pursuance of the divine order the planet Mercury "falls" in this thrice yearly circuit about the Lord of Day as the latter passes the sign of Libra, the highest of the 12.

The story of Solomon and his Temple is not a mere chronicle of historical events, but, employing actual events and personages of far less contemporary historical importance than represented, as the basis of fact, the transcendent literary and spiritual genius of Israel wove a marvelous fabric of Oriental splendor, the object of which was to display the glory of Jehovah in His Universe in such a manner as indelibly to impress it upon the minds of men for all time.

The symbolization of the Universe by means of a Temple edifice may be traced in the earliest Mesopotamian monuments. They were originally conceived as gigantic sundials constituted by erecting a circle of 12 upright stones around a central altar. These were the ancient Palestinian gilgals and were the patterns for the later Druidical circles. A study of their shadows enabled the priests to predict the changes in the seasons, knowledge extremely useful to agricultural and pastoral peoples. As time passed and knowledge increased, the forms of religious edifices were made to express this developed science. Their masses were outlined in angles which recorded the direction of the plane of the ecliptic, the earth's axis, and the equator, the elevation above the horizon of the polar star, and constellations heralding the equinoxes and solstices.

Far antedating the Pyramids of Egypt were the step pyramids or seven-storied zigurrats, as the Temple observatories were called among the Assyrians, Babylonians, and Chaldeans. They did not embody all the details of the Hebrew description, but they were the original "King Solomon's Temples."

A Short Explanation of the Seal of Solomon

By Albert G. Mackey

The Seal of Solomon or the Shield of David, for under both names the same thing was denoted, is a hexagonal figure consisting of two interlaced triangles, thus forming the outlines of a six-pointed star. Upon it was inscribed one of the sacred names of God, from which inscription it was opposed principally to derive its talismanic powers.

These powers were very extensive, for it was believed that it would extinguish fire, prevent wounds in a conflict, and perform many other wonders. The Jews called it the Shield of David in reference to the protection which it gave to its Possessors. But to we other Orientalists it was more familiarly known as the Seal of Solomon. Among these imaginative people, there was a very prevalent belief in the magical character of the King of Israel. He was esteemed rather as a great magician than as a great monarch, and by the signet which he wore, on which this talismanic seal was engraved, he is supposed to have accomplished the most extraordinary actions, and by it to have enlisted in his service the labors of the genii for the construction of his celebrated Temple.

Robinson Crusoe and the *Thousand and One Nights* are two books which every child has read, and which no man or woman ever forgets. In the latter are many allusions to Solomon's Seal. Especially is there a story of an unlucky fisherman who fished up in his net a bottle secured by a leaden stopper, on which this seal was impressed. On opening it, a fierce Afrite, or evil genii, came forth, who gave this account of the cause of his imprisonment. "*Solomon,*" said he, "*the son of David, exhorted me to embrace the faith and submit to his authority; but I refused; upon which he called for this bottle, and confined me in it, and closed it upon me with the leaden stopper and stamped upon it his seal, with the great name of God engraved upon it. Then he gave the vessel to one of the genii, who submitted to him, with orders to cast me into the sea.*"

Of all talismans, there is none, except, perhaps, the cross, which was so generally prevalent among the ancients as this Seal of Solomon or Shield of David. It has been found in the cave of Elephanta, in India, accompanying the image of the Deity, and many other places celebrated in the Brahmanical and the Buddhist religions. Hay, in an exploration into Western Barbary, found it in the harem of a Moor, and in a Jewish synagogue, where it was suspended in front of the recess in which the sacred rolls were deposited. In fact, the interlaced triangles or Seal of Solomon may be considered as par excellence, by merit, the great Oriental talisman.

In time, with the progress of the new religion, it ceased to be invested with a magical reputation, although the Hermetic philosophers of the Middle Ages did employ it as one of their mystical symbols; but true to the theory that superstitions may be repudiated but never will be forgotten, it was adopted by the Christians as one of the emblems of their faith, but with varying interpretations. The two triangles were said sometimes to be symbols of fire and water, sometimes of prayer and remission, sometimes of creation and redemption, or of life and death, or of resurrection and judgment. But at length the ecclesiologists seem to have settled on the idea that the figure should be considered as representing the two natures of our Lord—His Divine and His human nature.

Thus we find the Seal of Solomon dispersed all over Europe, in medallions, made at a very early period, on the breasts of the recumbent effigies of the dead as they lie in their tombs, and more especially in churches, where it is presented to us either carved on the walls or painted in the windows. Everywhere in Europe and now in the United States, where ecclesiastics architecture is beginning at length to find a development of taste, is this old Eastern talisman to be found doing its work as a Christian emblem. The spirit of the old talismanic faith is gone, but the form remains, to be nourished by us as the natural homage of the present to the past.

Among the old Cabalistic Hebrews, the Seal of Solomon was, as a talisman, of course deemed to be a sure preventive against the danger of fire. The more modern Jews, still believing in its talismanic virtues placed it as a safeguard on their houses and on other buildings, because they were especially liable to the danger of fire. The common people, seeing this figure affixed always to brew-houses, mistook it for a sign, and in time, in Upper Germany, the hexagon, or Seal of Solomon, was adopted by German innkeepers as the sign of a beer house, just as the chequers has been adopted in England, though with a different history, as the sign of a tavern.

King Solomon's Temple and the Story of the Third Degree

By Robert Smailes

Part I: The Building of the Temple

Before commencing the subject of my address, permit me to remind you of a question with which you are all familiar, from the very beginning of your Masonic career. I mean, "What is Freemasonry?" And the answer you are equally familiar with, "Freemasonry is a peculiar system of morality, veiled in allegory, and illustrated by symbols." Symbolism has been said to be the soul of Masonry, the ritual is the mere earthly wrapping in which it is enclosed; but while we recognize that Symbolism is the essential part of our Order, and that we are not bound to anything in particular, by the mere wording of the ritual, still it cannot be without interest to know something of the historical basis on which that ritual is founded; and though I cannot hope to invest the subject with the oriental picturesqueness which it deserves, I trust I shall not weary you, by giving a brief account of the events connected with the building of King Solomon's Temple, before considering the Story of the Third Degree.

Let us transport ourselves back in imagination to the time when King David, having become settled in his kingdom, and having built himself a palace at Jerusalem, felt it incongruous that the Ark of the Lord should be housed in wood and curtains; he was, therefore, desirous of building a suitable habitation for it; but he was not permitted to carry out his design. Yet he did everything that was possible to him; he collected stonemasons, and artificers, and amassed-according to the Book of Chronicles - 100,000 talents of gold, and 1,000,000 talents of silver, brass and iron without weight, and many precious stones.

These sums appear to have been much exaggerated, for nothing can be more futile than the attempt to show that such a Prince as David could have been able to amass gold, not to speak of other treasures, which amounted on the very lowest computation to £120,000,000 of our present money, and this exaggeration has had much to do with the doubts expressed by some writers, as to whether Solomon's Temple ever existed at all. Jewish tradition has accepted the most extravagant statements about the Temple, yet sober and trustworthy documents prove, that, though no larger than many an English Church, it was indeed, for that age, "exceedingly magnifical," and its fame spread to the furthest parts of the then known world, while it became an object of envy and emulation to the succeeding ages, so that 1500 years later the Emperor Justinian, when he had rebuilt the Church of St. Sophia at Constantinople, is said to have exclaimed "at last I have surpassed King Solomon."

David's difficulties were enormous, the Israelites were tent- dwellers and knew nothing of building, and he had not suitable timber at hand. Fortunately for him, to the north-west was the little country of Phoenicia, a narrow strip of land on the Syrian coast, towered over on the east by the Mountains of

Lebanon, on whose sunny slopes, vast quantities of cedar, cypress, fir, and other trees grew.

Though only a small nation, the Phoenicians were the great colonizers of the day, and excelled in all the arts. They were, however, lacking in food supplies, and had to look to Canaan for corn, wine, and oil. David had therefore no difficulty in forming a treaty with Hiram, King of Tyre, who, in return for the supplies he needed, was quite willing to let David have the timber and workmen he required.

Huge rafts of timber were floated by sea from Tyre to Joppa, a distance of 200 miles, and then with infinite toil, dragged about 35 miles up the steep and rocky roads to Jerusalem. This work was done by a large number of men, over whom overseers were appointed, and of these ADONIRAM was the chief. Adoniram, as you know, is a character of considerable Masonic importance as the reputed successor of Hiram Abiff. When his duties as overseer were completed, he was appointed by Solomon to the office of collector of tribute, or inland revenue officer, and he continued to fill this post until the death of the King. He was again appointed by Rehoboam, but the Israelites, who had put up with Solomon's extravagance, owing to his wisdom and reputation, now rebelled, and the venerable old man, grown grey in the service of his country, met with a different reception, for the cry had gone forth "To your tents, O Israel," and they stoned him with stones until he died.

Resuming the story of the Temple; on the death of David, his son Solomon continued the preparations for a further period of four years, when they were sufficiently advanced to allow of the building being commenced, and the King of Tyre again proved his friendship to Israel by sending HIRAM ABIFF to be the chief architect, a man whose skill-like that of Michael Angelo-seems to have been serviceable for every branch of art.

Mount Moriah was found to be a very difficult site for such a building; the sides of the hill were steep, its summit was rough and of insufficient size for the forecourts of the house. These courts had to be supported by immense walls, which have partly survived the ravages of many conquests. For the skilled work the King had to rely on Sidonian workmen, among whom special mention is made of the GIBLITES (stone-squarers), the people of Gebal, or Byblos, which was north of Berytos, and nearest to the Cedars of Lebanon. Ezekiel long afterwards mentions the wisdom and artistic genius of this Phoenician community. Even in Homer, the Sidonians are famed for embroidered robes, and skill in workmanship. In addition to so large a host of workmen, others were engaged in casting bronze in earthen molds; this was done in the clay soil of the Valley of Jordan, between Zarthan or Zeredathah, and Succoth, and the superintendent of all was HIRAM ABIFF.

The character of the architecture, both inside and out, was undoubtedly Phoenician. From Tyre, too, came the use of curtains, dyed in the scarlet juice of the trumpet-fish, and other costly dyes. We know that inside the Temple no stone was visible, all was of gilded cedar- wood, cypress, and olive, variously carved, and tapestried in parts by purple and embroidered hangings. Strangely enough, existing records leave us entirely in the dark as to the external appearance of the Temple, and it is unnecessary to go into the various speculations on the subject.

Let us try to represent, says Dean Farrar, what a visitor would have seen, had he been permitted to wander into the sacred courts and buildings of this most celebrated of earthly shrines. Passing through the thickly clustering houses of the Levites and the Porticoes, he might enter the Temple by one of the numerous gateways mentioned in the Book of Chronicles and elsewhere.

Two gates did Solomon construct, devoted to acts of mercy. Through one gate the bridegrooms used to pass, through the other the mourners. The people on the Sabbath rejoiced with the bridegrooms, and consoled the afflicted. These gates were of wood, overlaid with brass. When the visitor stood in the outer court, he would have seen on one side of the Temple area, a grove of trees, Olives, Palms, Cedars, and Cypresses, which added to the beauty of the building, but were afterwards abused for idolatrous purposes. To pass from the outer court, into the court which Jeremiah calls "the higher court," the visitor would have had to pass up some steps, through an enclosure built with three rows of hewn stones, supported by a cornice of Cedar beams. On the south-eastern side he would have admired the huge laver or basin, for the ablutions of the priests, which was regarded as one of the finest specimens of the skill of HIRAM ABIFF. It was made of brass, and was known as "the brazen or molten sea." It had a length and breadth of 45 feet, and stood 71/2 feet high, on the backs of 12 brazen oxen of the same height, of which three faced to each quarter of the heavens.

Approaching the porch, the eye would have been first caught by two superb pillars, which were regarded in those days as a miracle of art, and which for unknown reasons, received the name of Jachin and Boaz. Strange to say, it is a matter of dispute whether these two pillars stood detached from the porch, or were mere ornaments within it, or formed part of its absolute support, or, as is now believed by many, belonged to a detached gate in front of the porch itself. Ferguson, in his latest designs, supposed that the pillars were not detached like obelisks, but that they supported a screen or gateway, like the vine-bearing screen, described by Josephus and the Talmud, in front of the Temple of Herod. They were broken up and carried away, four centuries later, by the King of Babylon.

The Temple itself was surrounded on two sides by three stories of chambers. A winding stair led up into the middle chamber of the middle story, and thence into the upper story. These chambers communicated with each other, and were, according to Josephus, thirty in number; they were useful for a multitude of purposes; it does not appear that they were ever inhabited, but they served as store rooms for the priests' garments, and for the immense accumulations of Temple furniture. You will remember, it was up this winding staircase, our Ancient Fellow Craft Brethren are said to have gone to receive their wages.

I need not go further into the construction of the Temple, except to say that the holiest place was plunged in unbroken and perpetual gloom. It contained nothing but the Ark, and one or two other precious memorials of the Mosaic age.

The whole structure was completed in sacred silence. The awful sanctity of the shrine would have been violated, if its erection had been accompanied by the harsh and violent noises which would accompany the ordinary toil of masons; every stone and beam had been therefore carefully prepared beforehand, and was merely carried to its place, "so that neither was hammer, nor axe, nor any tool of iron heard in the house while it was building." The erection occupied seven-and-a-half years, in spite of the small size of the actual Temple. Size indeed, was no element of its magnificence, for, as I have said, it was much smaller than many an English Church. But it must be remembered it was not intended for either priests or worshippers. Ancient and Eastern worship was mainly in the open air; the Shrine itself only symbolized the residence of God.

And so the Temple was completed, and after a further period of twelve months, for preparation, came the most magnificent ceremony the nation had ever known, viz. the Dedication, culminating in the beautiful prayer of Solomon, with the constantly recurring refrain, "Hear, Thou in Heaven, Thy dwelling-place, and when Thou hearest, Lord, forgive."

"Sacred to Heaven behold the dome appears, "Lo, what august solemnity it wears. "Angels themselves have deigned to deck the fane, "And beauteous Sheba shall proclaim its fame."

The Temple was thenceforth the center of all the national life of the Jews, and that center was no idol shrine, no material image, but the symbolic palace of Him, whom Heaven and the Heaven of Heavens could not contain.

Passing over the visit of the Queen of Sheba, we must carry the history of Solomon a little farther; he continued his building operations for a period of twenty years, at the end of which time the King of Tyre thought they ought to have a squaring-up, when it was found that Solomon was considerably indebted to him, and also that the exchequer was empty. Solomon, however, made Hiram a present of some country next to Phoenicia with which at first Hiram was very pleased, but when he went to view it, he found it worthless, and that he had been over-reached. Notwithstanding this diplomatic breeze, no breach appears to have been made in the friendship of the two Kings.

Jewish writers in less ancient times cannot overlook HIRAM'S uncircumcision in his services towards building the Temple. Their legends relate, that because he was a God-fearing man, and built the Temple, he was received alive into Paradise, but that after he had been there a thousand years, he sinned by pride, and was thrust down into hell.

You will notice, that while we have this legend about the KING of TYRE, and the authentic record of the death of ADONIRAM by stoning, there is nothing to indicate the end of HIRAM ABIFF. It has been urged by some that there were two architects, father and son, and that the father was killed as stated in our ritual, and succeeded by the son. This theory is based on what I think is a wrong translation of the word "Abiff," and occurs in the message from the KING OF TYRE to SOLOMON: "And now I have sent a cunning man, endued with understanding of Hiram, my father's." Abiff is a compound name: "Ab," meaning "father," is a token of respect, and "I," or "If," the definite article, and is not intended merely in the parental sense, as Abraham, the father of the faithful, but Abiff is more properly the father or master builder. I think we are bound to conclude there was only one great architect for the Temple, and this prototype of our Order disappears very modestly from view in the simple words recorded in the Book of Chronicles, "And HIRAM finished the work he had to make for KING SOLOMON for the House of God."

And now we will change the scene from this vision of Eastern splendor, to the more somber atmosphere of London, at the beginning of the eighteenth century, when four Lodges, meeting at such quaint houses as "The Goose and Gridiron," "The Rummer and Grapes," the "Apple Tree Tavern," and the "Crown Ale-house," decided to form themselves into a GRAND LODGE in order to reform and reorganize Freemasonry in accordance with the spirit of the age, of which Lodge ANTHONY SAYER was elected Grand Master in 1717.

Of the men who took part in this reorganization, the three most eminent were Dr. Theoph. Desaguliers, the Rev. James Anderson, and George Payne. Payne was the second Grand Master in 1718. Anderson was afterwards asked to write the Book of Constitutions. Desaguliers was third Grand Master, and of this triumvirate, probably the most important.

He was the son of a French Protestant Minister, and was born at Rochelle in 1683. After the edict of Nantes, he with his father came to London in 1685. His education was finished at Oxford, and in the course of time he attained considerable notoriety as a mathematician and natural philosopher. In 1705 he gave a course of public lectures on experimental philosophy, which were attended by persons of all classes of society. In 1723 he was commissioned by Parliament to devise a plan for heating and ventilating the House of Commons, which he effected in a very ingenious manner. There are some occurrences in the life of Desaguliers which merit particular attention, as having exercised a peculiar influence on the Masonry of his day. His love of mechanics, and the prominent part which that science plays in operative Masonry, no doubt induced him to become a member of the Fraternity. He soon, however, found the Brethren could teach him nothing. On the other hand, the spirit of toleration which he found prevailing among the members of the Fraternity, peculiarly grateful to one who had suffered from religious intolerance, inspired him with the idea of reconstructing the Society on a basis which should unite together in harmony, those who were divided by religious and political schisms. In carrying out his plan, he was materially aided by the high position he held in society, and by the widespread acquaintance he enjoyed. As a French refugee he was, of course, a zealous Protestant, and this fact must have influenced him in making alterations in the ritual of Masonry, in which several changes were made subsequent to 1717, for the purpose of divesting it of some of the lingering remnants of Romanism.

Of these changes, the most important was the fundamental one which is at the root of our present system that of belief. You will remember the old Charges all began with an invocation to the Trinity; later this seems to have been changed to God and the Holy Church; the latter was now dropped, and a simple belief in the Deity only imposed on initiates. One cannot help thinking that the leaders of the movement belonged to the Latitudinarian School of Theology, as this school was distinguished from both Puritans and High Churchmen by their opposition to dogma, and by their preference of reason to tradition, an example of which we have in that beautiful portion of the ritual, where we are forcibly impressed to "listen to the dictates of reason."

Part II:

The Story of the Third Degree

The Story of the Third Degree is a philosophical essay on Death, in which is recited the supposed death of Hiram Abiff, at or about the completion of King Solomon's Temple, and just as it is the sum of the small which makes the large, and a simple word may plant the seed which, in its time, blossoms into fragrant action, and alters the courses of lives, rounding life itself into its fullest beauty, so this tragedy of the Tyrian architect has blossomed into an Order, whose branches are extended over the whole surface of the habitable globe, and of which we are justly proud.

We have seen, however, that there is no historical foundation for this story, and I have it on the authority of Bro. HUGHAN, that ritualistically HIRAM ABIFF is unknown before the THIRD DEGREE, and this has not been traced before 1723-7. Many eminent Masons have sought for the story in the Miracle Plays of the Middle Ages, but without success. The question then arises, Was the story entirely originated by the compilers of the new ritual, or was there some foundation for it existing in the CRAFT GUILDS before the formation of GRAND LODGE?

It is not to be supposed that Brethren, who a generation later, split up on very simple points into Ancients and Moderns, would allow an entirely new legend to be introduced into

Freemasonry, and I think there is sufficient evidence to prove that some story of HIRAM, the Builder, was known to Masons before this period.

In the account of the Installation of the DUKE OF MONTAGU as Grand Master in 1721, we read that immediately afterwards, as if unpremeditatedly, the Grand Master Montagu nominated Dr. John Beal, Deputy Grand Master, who was invested and installed into the chair of HIRAM ABIFF, to the left hand of the Grand Master.

Professor Swift Johnson has made a study of the literature of the 17th century, with a view of tracing the introduction of the legend during that period, but without success. In a paper read before the Q.C. Lodge, he says:

"As a result of such search as I have made in the subject put before you, we may safely conclude that in the 17th century, the description of King Solomon's Temple excited a very considerable amount of attention and interest; but that in the writings that appeared, there was little, if anything, of Masonic importance. The result may be called a failure, were it not that we should always bear in mind the sound Baconian maxim, that the negative instance is always more valuable than the positive. It shows that the legends were not taken wholesale into our system from an outside source of current knowledge, and leaves us with the alternative that this characteristic of our Craft was either part and parcel of the ancient teaching, or that it was an addition made at or about the beginning of modern Masonry."

Looking further back, we find that in the first English Bible, published by Coverdale in 1535, Hiram, the architect, is there spoken of as Hiram Abiff, but in all the succeeding translations the "Abiff" is omitted, and only reappears to our knowledge in Masonry in 1721, so it is fair to presume, it had been handed down orally, through the Masons from the former time.

Then there is what is known as Dr. MARKS' wonderful discovery. Dr. Marks was not a Mason, but a celebrated Hebrew scholar, and in his researches at Oxford, he came across an Arabic Manuscript of the 14th century, in which reference is made to a Masonic sign or password, and which, translated, would read, "We have found our Lord Hiram." Bro. Hughan writes me, "Long before such an announcement, a Jewish Rabbi explained just such a reading to Capt. Philips 33° and myself."

Looking abroad for evidence, we find in France a Society called "Les Companions du tour de France," which was divided into three, "Sons of Solomon," "Pere Soubise," and "Maitre Jacques," and included other trades besides Masons. PERDIGUIER, a French writer, informs us "that the joiners of Maitre Jacques wear white gloves, because, as they say, they did not steep their hands in the blood of Hiram." Also apropos of "chien," a title bestowed on some of the Companions, he says, "It is believed by some, to be derived from the fact, that it was a dog which discovered the place where the body of Hiram, the Architect of the Temple, lay under the rubbish; after which, all the Companions who separated from the murderers of Hiram, were called 'chiens' or dogs."

I think you will agree that we have some evidence of a legend of the death of Hiram existing before Grand Lodge era. When could such a tale have been incorporated into Medieval Masonry? The late Bro. SPETH once said:

"I can see no epoch more likely than that of the return from the Crusades. The Knights of the Cross were enthusiastic builders ; the remains of their Churches dot the Holy Land to this day. The European builders must, in the nature of things, have required large numbers of native workmen to assist them, and among these the Temple legend, if it existed, would certainly be known. The builders, on their return, would have brought the legend with them, and it would have been adopted all the more readily, as it was in perfect accord with the traditions, aye, even of the practices, of that age in England."

Another factor in the construction of the Story of the Third Degree was the exhibition of a large model of King Solomon's Temple in London, in 1724.

As Prof. Swift Johnson has told us, the Temple seems to have captivated the imagination of a large number of writers during the 17th century, both in England and on the continent. Among the latter, a Spanish Jesuit, called VILLALPANDUS, was the most eminent. In obedience to a royal command, he drew up a description of the Temple, and regarding the plan as being given by the Most High to the wisest of Kings, he incorporated in his account all those excellencies he deemed essential to a most perfect edifice; and this description was practically repeated by Bishop WALTON in his polyglot Bible, published in 1657. Partly in opposition to this description,

SAMUEL LEE published his "Orbis Miraculum," or the Temple of Solomon portrayed by Scripture light, and this is interesting to us, because we read for the first time of a symbolic meaning attached to the two pillars, B. and J. He says:

"The pillar on the right side, that is, the South, was called Jachin-He shall establish, noting the fixedness of the pillar on its foundation ; and that on the left hand, or on the North side, was called Boaz, denoting the strength and firmitude of that piece of brass."

JOHN LIGHTFOOT, one of the giants of Biblical criticism, was the first to translate the results of his Hebrew reading into the vernacular, and sums up his account of the Temple in these words:

"And indeed Solomon's Temple did very truly resemble one of our Churches, but only that it differeth in this, that the steeple of it (which was in the porch) stood at the east end."

Hugh Broughton, John Selden a lawyer, John Ogilby, and towards the end of the century, Humphrey Prideaux Dean of Norwich, all had something to say on the subject.

I have quoted these writers to explain the interest which was taken in the exhibition of this model in 1724. A handbook to it was published in 1725, a copy of which is in the possession of Bro. W. H. RYLANDS, from which I will quote the following extracts:

"The Temple of Solomon, with all its Porches, Walls, Gates, Halls, Chambers, Holy Vessels, the Altar of Burnt Offering, the Molten Sea, Golden Candlesticks, Shew Bread

Tables, Altar of Incense, the Ark of the Covenant, with the Mercy Seat, the Cherubim, &c."

"The motive of forming this model of Solomon's Temple, which is now seen here in London, was an Opera, representing the Destruction of Jerusalem, acted at Hamborough, and as the Opera House was built at the charge of Councilor Schott, a man very learned and judicious, much renowned for the pains he took to represent his scenes in the most accurate manner, and altogether to conform to antiquity. The last decoration of the before-mentioned Opera, where the City of Jerusalem, together with the Temple, are represented, was brought by him to the highest degree of perfection. The project thereof was not carried on, by opinion or conceit, but according to the direction of the Scriptures, and the most authentic authors, not neglecting to consult in all points thereon, the most renowned architects and learned men then living."

You can quite understand that this Exhibition soon won its way to popular favor, and cannot have been without effect on the rank and file of Freemasons at the very time when our legends were being molded and harmonized, and this model must have exercised a real influence in the development of our ritual.

Bro. JOHN SENEX, the publisher of the first Book of Constitutions, in 1723, in which year he was junior Grand Warden, also published a finely executed engraving, or plan of Jerusalem, with views of the Temple and its principal ornaments. This publication, by one of the Grand Officers, could not. fail to have extensive circulation among the Lodges. The setting of such legends as had to do with the Temple, must have been so framed as to accord with the impression left by an engraving, that might fairly be regarded as semiofficial.

We have, then, the dry bones of a legend of the death of Hiram, and the exhibition of this model as a fitting "mise en scene" for the Story of the Third Degree, but what was the power, whence came the vital force which put life into these dry bones, caused the Courts of the Temple to resound once more with the feet of moving masses of workmen, and produced the beautiful ritual, as we now have it?

Let us turn for a moment to consider the social condition of England at the time this new ritual was promulgated. The first of the new line of Hanoverian Kings reigned on the throne, a king who knew not the language, and cared less for the people, and whose Court was presided over by two of his German mistresses. The real ruler of the kingdom was Robert Walpole, a clever, but corrupt statesman, who kept himself in power for over twenty years by bribing the House of Commons. Of the prominent statesmen of the time, the greater part were unbelievers in any form of Christianity, and distinguished for the grossness and immorality of their lives. The Church was at its lowest ebb, in that deepest darkness of the gloom which preceded the dawn of the revival by Whitfield and the Wesleys; its ministers were the most remiss in their duties and the least severe in their lives, and to talk of religion was to be laughed at.

The philosophy of the day was that of HOBBES and his disciples, one of whom declared the Soul was only a state of nervous vibrations, and HOBBES taught that friendship was only a sense of social utility to one another. The so-called laws of nature, such as gratitude or the love of our neighbor, were, in fact, contrary to the natural passions of man, and powerless to restrain them.

Both the high and the low were drunken and licentious, and the pictures of Hogarth, which we are inclined to look upon as caricatures, were true pictures of the life of that day. The little leaven was only to be found in the middle classes.

We can well believe, that to such an intelligent and enlightened philosopher as Desaguliers appears to have been, such a social condition must have been most repulsive.

The Landmarks of the Order are a standing protest against atheism for all time. The ritual of the Third Degree was an active protest against the irreligion and immorality of the day.

How different the teaching of our ritual from that of Lord Chesterfield in his celebrated letters to his son, written about this time, in which he instructed him in the art of seduction, as part of a polite education. Compare the philosophy of which I have spoken with "Listen to the dictates of reason, which teach you that even in this vile and perishable frame, there exists a vital and immortal principle." Contrast Death, represented as a skeleton with a scythe-the avenging angel, the fell destroyer-with "the holy and inspiring hope which will enable you to trample the king of terrors beneath your feet."

Brethren, I have no documentary evidence in support of this theory, and nowadays nothing is accepted in Masonry without it; formerly the wildest fables were advanced to prove the antiquity of the Order, but "tempora mutantur," we have changed all that, and the pendulum has swung all the other way, perhaps it has swung too far; documentary evidence is not always to be relied on, -the kings of England were described in official and other documents as Kings of France long after they had lost all power in that country, and other instances could be quoted.

At any rate the ritual was not at once popular, and Masters' Lodges were formed for working it, while it was not until twenty years later it was compulsory, and properly incorporated with the making of a Mason. I will not speak of the opposition of the Gormogons, [A brotherhood somewhat similar to Freemasons, which existed in England between 1725 and 1738.] nor pursue this view of the Story of the Third Degree further, but will rather leave it to your earnest consideration, and, in conclusion, return to the point from which we started, viz. : The Symbolism of Masonry, and though we may not be able to trace with certainty the origin of our Order, nor the exact source of its ritual, the Soul of Masonry will live if we ever remember the three grand principles on which it is founded: "BROTHERLY LOVE," "RELIEF," and "TRUTH," and never forget that "Death has no terrors equal to the stain of falsehood and dishonor."

www.ingramcontent.com/pod-product-compliance
Lightning Source LLC
LaVergne TN
LVHW041458070426
835507LV00009B/664